MOONSHINE MAKING FOR BEGINNERS

Step by step guide on how to make moonshine liquor recipes at home

AF490501

Marie Kraus

Table of content

CHAPTER ONE

INTRODUCTION

Everybody can make home brew and yes a little learning goes far on the off chance that you are absolutely new in it. Nonetheless, it takes expertise and some experience to make the best. Preferably, you should do it again and again, with some improvement each time you are busy to consummate your art. Also, the pride of keeping this rich culture alive is very satisfying if not altogether exciting.

First of all, home brew is made through a process known as distillation. Before you begin , note that it is illicit to distil spirits at home and this article is strictly for instructive purposes.

What is distillation?

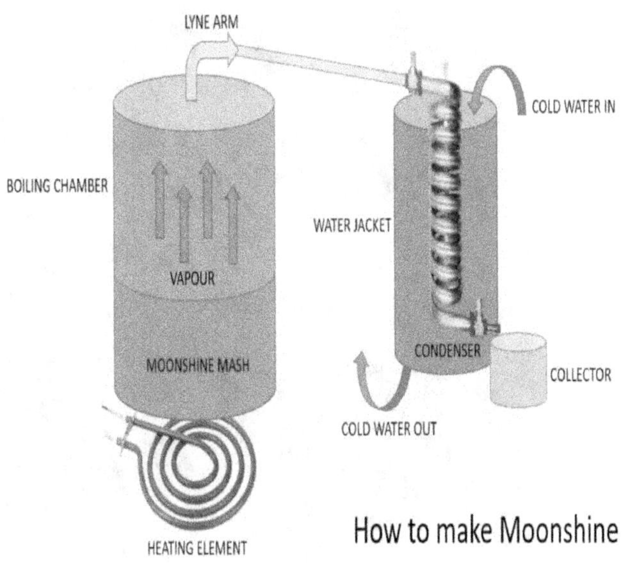

How to make Moonshine

distilling is defined as a method
of separating parts of a fluid
substance based on the different
boiling point of the substance.
The result of distilling is complete
or partial seperation of segments

where the concentration of the chose segments increases. For home brew, the refining cycle isolates ethanol from water making the convergence of ethanol more grounded.

When making home brew, refining is normally the last interaction. Refining is done on effectively arranged and aged crush. This is done to separate ethanol. Ethanol has an edge of boiling over of 172 °F (77 °C) which is lower than that of water which is 212 °F (100 °C). At the point when the mash is heated, ethanol will be quick to bubble and disintegrate, a cycle that isolates it from water. It is then removed by gathering the fume and gathering it in a container.

CHAPTER TWO

Making Moonshine

Stage 1: Materials needed

Before you start any process, it is important to set up your required materials for the procedure. These include:

- Fermentation container
- Boiling pot
- Heat source
- Airlock
- Glass container
- Hydrometer
- Steel
- Fire extinguinsher

•Fermentation compartment:

The compartment is the place

where you'll keep your pound and
give it an opportunity to age.

- **Airlock**: Normally made of
  plastic, this gadget permits
  carbon dioxide to escape

from the fermentation container and preventing air from entering the compartment hence keeping the mash from oxidation

•**Heat source**: Wood, gas, and power are three source of heat ordinarily used during distillation

•Boiling pot: Utilized for heating water for getting ready mash.

•**Steel:** A copper or tempered steel actually makes a decent choice and make certain to get the correct size i.e going between 5-8-gallon (19-30-liter)still

•**Temperature measure**: For estimating the temperature inside the still

•**Hydrometer:** A gadget that measures the thickness[density] of a fluid in relation to water. You will require both the brewing hydrometer for fermentation and distilling hydrometer for use during distillation.

•**Fire extinguisher**: You will utilize heat consequently have a plan B fire extinguisher for safety measure.

•**Collection holders**: Have some glass containers in which your spirit will be gathered and stored

CHAPTER THREE

Stage 2: making the mash
To make the mash you will require

- 5 gallons (18.9 liters) of water

- 8.5 pounds (3.9 kg) flaked corn

- 1.5 pounds (0.5 kg) squashed malted grain

- Yeast

Technique[procedure]

1. Start by heating the 5 gallons (18.9 liters) of water in the fermented holder to 165 °F (73.9 °C).

2. Turn off the heat and pour in the 8.5 pounds (3.9 kg) of flaked corn while mixing continuously for about 5 minutes. After this, mix the combination at regular intervals as you check the temperature

and stop when the temperature drops to 152 °F (66.7 °C).

3.   Now, pour in the 1.5 pounds (0.5 kg) of squashed malted grain and cover the compartment for 1.5 hours while open it after at regular intervals at every fifteen 15minute to mix the combination.

4.   Let the combination sit for an additional 2 hours or so to permit it to cool to 70 °F (21 °C).

5.   Add in the yeast and expose the mixture by turning it over persistently between two pots until you are certain the yeast has blended in well. Your squash

is arranged and hanging tight for the following cycle which is fermentation.

Stage 3: Fermentation

•	Once your squash is very much circulated air through, cover the pot and let it sit at room temperature for at any rate fourteen days. Note that yeast works best at room temperature in this manner continue to screen the temperature to ensure it doesn't get excessively low.

•	During fermentation, utilize your hydrometer to gauge gravity both toward the beginning and toward the finish of the fourteen days. If all else fails, you can give the cycle another week to ensure that all sugars have been separated. Your squash should deliver the smell of liquor before the finish of the three weeks.

•	Strain the mash through clean cheesecloth to seprate the solid substance from the mash fluid. This fluid ought to have a pH of 6.0. In the event that lower, add a little calcium carbonate to bring it up.if it is higher, add some citrus extract to cut it down.

CHAPTER FOUR

Stage 4: Distillation

With your mash water, it is presently an ideal opportunity to make your home brew. This progression is unquestionably less including contrasted with setting up the mash and indeed, you should be energized and happy having come this far. Also, coming this far and prepared to continue must be that you are doing this legitimately or so we trust.

- Distilling is essentially creating cleansed liquor out of your mash water. ensure that your still is completely cleaned up prior to utilizing it. There are different kinds of stills with various highlights and activity modes. Any actually should accompany a working manual on buy which will give you rules on care, preparing, and use.

•   Setting up your still ought to include loading it with copper cross section to proof the liquor as well as interfacing your water info and yield if your still has a condenser. Loading with copper network makes a reflux in the segment while additionally responding with sulfur mixtures to dispose of them bringing about an incredible preference for your home brew [moonshine].

- Once this is done, add your stressed mash water into the still. To this point, ensure only pure and clean liquor fluid gets into the still. If all else fails, think about stressing this fluid by and by through a cheesecloth to wipe out residue.

Stage 5: Running the still

Note that you now have your liquor[alcohol] from the mash. The reason for the distillation procedure is to seperate your liquor from different mixtures in your mash fluid. Turn your source of heat on and bring the temperature up to 150 °F (65.6 °C) at that point turn on your condensing water. It will begin dribbling on the condenser to cool it. As it does, increment the heat until the previously run of distillate is created. This ought to be at around 190-200 °F (87.8-93.3 °C) temperature. Presently turn down the heat until you notice your distillate trickling consistently at 3-5 dribbles each second. At the point when this is accomplished, keep up your heat at this temperature.

CHAPTER FIVE

Stage 6: Collecting your distillate

In a perfect world, you should gather the distillate when it begins dribbling consistently. Alert, never utilize a plastic compartment to gather your distillate since it contains BPA which can debase your distillate. it is wise to utilize a glass compartment.

distillation happens in stages as clarified beneath.

- Foreshots

Also, gather and dispose of the first about 5% of your distillate.

This is known as foreshot and may contain methanol and different congeners which is dangerous to ingest as it is known to cause visual deficiency.

- Heads

After the foreshots, the following 30% of your distillate which is not pure but rather less risky compared with the foreshots is known as the heads. The heads highlight a trademark smell and unpredictable substances like CH3)2CO, acetic acid derivation, and acetaldehyde which makes its taste not all that great. It ought to likewise be spilled out and not devoured.

- Hearts

As the name proposes, this is the core of your distillate and the best as it is pure ethanol with neither foreign substances nor the smell found in the heads. The hearts will be the following 30% of the distillate.

- Tails

As you reach the finish of the distillation process, into the last 35% of your distillate, you will gather the tails. It takes some insight to cut the heads from the hearts and the hearts from the tail. With time and practice, you ought to accomplish this by both your feeling of smell and taste.

The tails taste fairly level without the rich taste of corn found in the heart. The tail contains starches and proteins just as fusel oils like butanol and propanol which gives it a slick elusive feel on your fingers. You have the alternative of disposing of the tails or refining it further.

Stage 7: Cleaning after

Whenever you are finished with the tails, your still will be emptied . Strip off the copper cross section and absorb your segment vinegar. When done, clean your still and dry it completely prior to putting away it away. Similarly, clean your thermometers, holders, and hydrometer and store them.

Try not to throw away your copper network at this time. You could utilize multiple times more. Tidy it up, dry it completely, and save it for the following use.

CHAPTER SIX

Conclusion

When making home brew at home, here are a few hints to notice.

- Making liquor inside can be hazardous. Home brew ought to be made out in the open if conceivable utilizing wood fire almost a waterpoint. This is additionally fitting since pound will in general have a solid horrendous smell which may wait inside days after you have arranged your sparkle.

- The best yeast to use for your pound is the brewer's yeast.

Others are known to create methanol which causes visual deficiency and at last demise whenever ingested.

•	Sour squash ought to be covered yet not firmly covered.

•	Don't avoid drawing in a coach on the off chance that you are on the correct side of the law. There is no damage in straightening the expectation to learn and adapt.

Moreover, you can likewise master preparing and distilling through

Most ideal approach to store home brew

Store the home brew crush in sealed shut glass containers. Ensure the glass containers are sterile and clean. Keep them in a cool, dim spot, fixed tight. You would then be able to taste home brew pound all alone or add it to mixed drinks and different beverages. Home brew crush should keep going for in any event a half year 1 year, whenever put away appropriately.

www.ingramcontent.com/pod-product-compliance
Lightning Source LLC
Chambersburg PA
CBHW060929130726
48001CB00006B/2483